SH!ARKS

MELISSA GISH

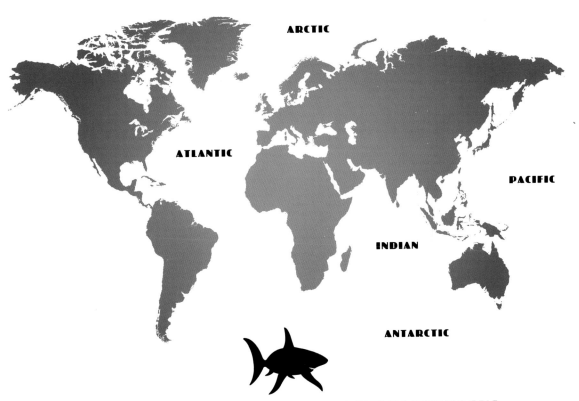

ARCTIC

ATLANTIC

PACIFIC

INDIAN

ANTARCTIC

CREATIVE EDUCATION · CREATIVE PAPERBACKS

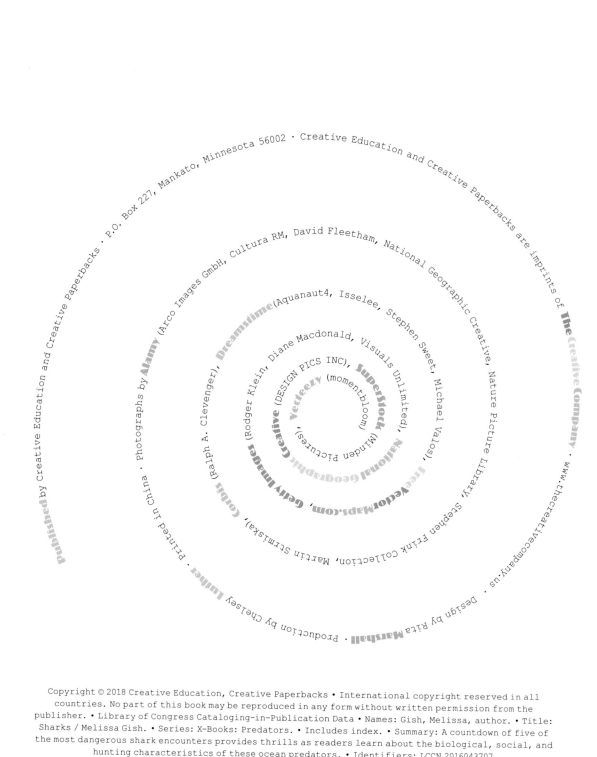

Published by Creative Education and Creative Paperbacks · P.O. Box 227, Mankato, Minnesota 56002 · Creative Education and Creative Paperbacks are imprints of **The Creative Company** · www.thecreativecompany.us · Design by Rita Marshall · Production by Chelsey Luther · Printed in China · Photographs by **Alamy** (Arco Images GmbH, Cultura RM, David Fleetham, National Geographic Creative, Nature Picture Library, Stephen Frink Collection, Martin Strmiska), **Corbis** (Ralph A. Clevenger), **Dreamstime** (Aquanaut4, Isselee, Stephen Sweet, Michael Valos), **Getty Images** (Rodger Klein, Diane Macdonald, Visuals Unlimited), **Creative** (DESIGN PICS INC), **National Geographic Creative**, **freevectormaps.com**, **Superstock** (Minden Pictures), **Vecteezy** (momentbloom)

• Library of Congress Cataloging-in-Publication Data • Names: Gish, Melissa, author. • Title: Sharks / Melissa Gish. • Series: X-Books: Predators. • Includes index. • Summary: A countdown of five of the most dangerous shark encounters provides thrills as readers learn about the biological, social, and hunting characteristics of these ocean predators. • Identifiers: LCCN 2016043707 ISBN 978-1-60818-821-5 (hardcover) • ISBN 978-1-62832-424-2 (pbk) • ISBN 978-1-56660-869-5 (eBook) Subjects: LCSH: Sharks—Juvenile literature. • Classification: LCC QL638.9.G57 2017 / DDC 597.3—dc23 CCSS: RI.3.1–8; RI.4.1–5, 7; RI.5.1–3, 8; RI.6.1–2, 4, 7; RH.6–8.3–8 First Edition HC 9 8 7 6 5 4 3 2 1 • First Edition PBK 9 8 7 6 5 4 3 2 1

SHARKS!

CONTENTS

PREDATORS BOOKS

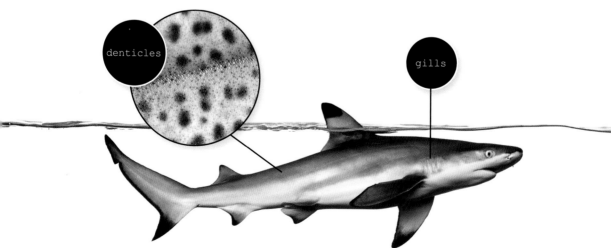

denticles

gills

XCEPTIONAL FISH

Sharks are fast and powerful swimmers. They have razor-sharp teeth. They have keen senses. Nearly 500 different kinds of sharks exist. Some are shy and calm. Others are ferocious predators.

Shark Basics

Sharks live in all of Earth's oceans. Some sharks also live in rivers. Sharks have unique bodies. Their skeletons are not made of bone. Instead, they are made of rubbery tissue called cartilage. This makes shark bodies lightweight. Sharks can speed through the water. They can turn sharply.

Sharks breathe through slits in their bodies called gills. Their skin is covered with tiny toothlike scales called denticles. They have three to six rows of sharp teeth in their powerful jaws.

WORLDWIDE SHARKS

= range of whale shark

dwarf lanternshark
territory

THE DWARF LANTERNSHARK

is the smallest known shark. Found only

in the southern Caribbean Sea, it is

about 8 inches (20.3 cm) long.

FEMALE SHARKS

are usually bigger than male sharks.

GREAT WHITES

can grow to 21 feet (6.4 m)

long and weigh 5,000

pounds (2,268 kg).

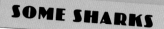

SOME SHARKS

grow as many as 50,000 teeth in a lifetime. Great whites can have teeth three inches (7.6 cm) long.

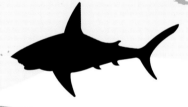

WHALE SHARKS,

the largest fish in the world, are up to 50 feet (15.2 m) long and more than 40,000 pounds (18,144 kg).

The dorsal fin runs along the shark's spine. Most sharks have two dorsal fins.

A shark's denticles and teeth get worn and broken. New denticles and teeth grow to replace old ones.

SHARK VISION

Sharks can see 10 times better than humans in low light.

Sharks are carnivores. This means they eat meat. Animals killed by predators are called prey. Sharks sense prey with their whole bodies. Tiny jelly-filled pits on the face sense the energy of swimming prey. These pits are called the ampullae of Lorenzini. Sharks also have a system of **organs** in their bodies called a lateral line. These organs help sharks follow prey's movement. Sharks can smell blood, too. These predators can find prey in total darkness.

Long ago, sailors nicknamed sharks "sea dogs."

SEA DOGS

SHARK BASICS FACT

Two kinds of sharks can live in rivers.

These are bull sharks and river sharks.

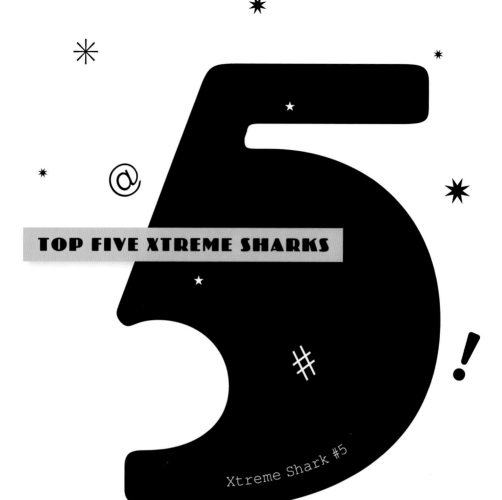

Xtreme Shark #5

Shark Bait In 1963, Rodney Fox was spearfishing in South Australian waters. Suddenly, a great white shark grabbed him. The shark's teeth tore open Rodney's abdomen and crushed his ribs. His lung was ripped open. Organs and arteries were pierced. The shark spit out Rodney and swam away. Rodney was rescued. He needed 462 stitches in his chest and 92 in his right hand and arm. Later, Rodney became a shark expert and conservationist.

On average, sharks kill fewer than six people per year.

But dangerous encounters can occur where sharks are present.

Shark Babies

Baby sharks are called pups. Most shark mothers carry eggs inside their bodies. The eggs hatch. Then the pups grow inside their mother for 6 to 22 months. Large sharks need more time to grow than small sharks.

Some sharks lay eggs in sea grass. Shark eggs are leathery pouches. Some are oddly shaped with twists and curves. They have vine-like growths called tendrils. Mother sharks hide their eggs from predators. The tendrils hold the eggs in the sea grass. Shark pups break out of the eggs after seven to nine months.

A few sharks give birth the way dogs and cats do. Pups form inside their mothers' bodies. They grow for six to seven months. Then they are born. Parent sharks do not feed their young. Pups come into the world ready to hunt. Many are big enough to defend themselves. Others hide until they grow bigger.

1 month

before birth

Develop fins and open eyes

1 foot (0.3 m)　**5** feet (1.5 m)

Two to 20 pups born

12 years
Begin hunting

15 years
Reproduce

1 day

Blue sharks can give birth to as many as 120 pups every year.

TOP FIVE XTREME SHARKS

Xtreme Shark #4

Targeted In 2007, Todd Endriss sat on his surfboard off the coast of Monterey, California. Dolphins swam nearby. A 15-foot (4.6 m) great white shark chomped Todd's body and surfboard like a sandwich. The shark's teeth shredded Todd's back. Then the shark bit Todd's leg. The dolphins rushed to Todd. They encircled him and chased the shark away. Todd needed 500 stitches and 200 staples. Six weeks later, he went surfing again.

XTRAORDINARY LIFESTYLE

Sharks are smart. Many travel the world's oceans. They remember the best feeding grounds. They sometimes work together to hunt. The largest sharks have no enemies. They are feared predators.

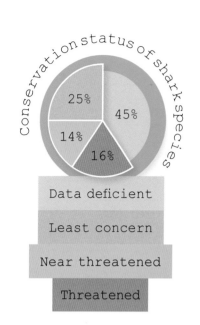

Conservation status of shark species

25%
45%
14%
16%

Data deficient

Least concern

Near threatened

Threatened

SHARK SOCIETY FACT

Tiger sharks patrol coral reefs.

They often attack Caribbean reef sharks (pictured).

Sharks swim about two miles (3.2 km) per hour.

SHARKS X ARE FAST

Shark Society

Coral reefs are home to a variety of sharks. Different **species** get along peacefully. They eat fish and **crustaceans** living on the reef. Other sharks roam the oceans alone. They hunt for larger prey.

A food source can draw many sharks to it. When sharks feed together, they get excited. They bite wildly at anything within reach. This is called a feeding frenzy. During a feeding frenzy, sharks often bite each other.

Even sharks that do not live on reefs visit them. They arrive once or twice a year. They do this to get cleaned. Small fish nibble the sharks' bodies and gills. They pick off dead tissue and slime. They eat **parasites**. They even clean food from between sharks' teeth. Sharks like being cleaned.

XEMPLARY SKILLS

Sharks can smell blood in water up to three miles (4.8 km) away. When sharks catch prey, they do not chew. They rip off chunks of meat and swallow them whole.

The sleeper shark can live under floating ice near the North and South poles.

Some sharks hunt in groups. Cow sharks use teamwork to kill whales. They swim in a tight circle around the prey. The prey cannot escape. Then the sharks attack. Blacktip reef sharks trap schools of fish this way.

Big sharks hunt fatty prey such as seals and sea lions. Tiger sharks are vicious hunters. They slam into prey. Then they rip the stunned animal to pieces. Great white sharks silently swim under prey. Then they rush straight up. Their jaws clamp down and crush prey. Sometimes great whites swim so fast that they launch out of the water.

TYPES OF TEETH

Wedge-shaped teeth with jagged edges — rip chunks of meat

Thin, knife-shaped teeth — catch and hold fish

Flattened teeth — crush shellfish

Xtreme Shark #3

Missing Leg In 1964, Henri Bource was swimming off southern Australia. He and some friends were filming seals. Suddenly, a great white shark rushed toward Henri. It seized his leg and shook him. The shark bit through Henri's knee and swam away with his leg. Henri's friends caught the encounter on film. Henri survived. Five years later, he used the film in a documentary about sharks called *Savage Shadows*.

XASPERATING CONFLICT

About half of all human encounters with sharks involve surfers. The rest of the time, sharks are being caught for food or sport.

Shark Survival

Humans kill nearly 100 million sharks every year. Yet, only a handful of species are very dangerous to humans. They include bull, tiger, and great white sharks. The number of sharks in the world keeps going down. But the number of times people encounter sharks has been going up. Sharks' behavior is changing. Scientists believe people are causing the changes.

One of the biggest causes is overfishing. This is when people take too many fish from an area. The fish cannot reproduce fast enough to bring their numbers back up. Humans have overfished many places. This leaves sharks with less food in their normal hunting grounds. They must come closer to shore to find food.

Great whites need to eat about 66 pounds (29.9 kg) of food every two weeks. Sharks do not hunt people. But if a person looks like food, sharks may bite him or her.

Among people trying to protect sharks, shark finning is another cause for concern. This is when sharks are caught and their fins are sliced off. They drown. Finning is banned in some countries. But where it is legal, sharks are in danger. They cannot swim without their fins. The sharks are then dumped back into the water.

SHARK SURVIVAL FACT

Tiger sharks can live 50 years. Whale sharks can live to age 100.

Xtreme Shark #2

Surf & Turf In 2003, 13-year-old Bethany Hamilton was surfing off the Hawaiian island of Kauai. Lying on her surfboard, she dangled her arm in the water. Without warning, a 14-foot (4.3 m) tiger shark bit off her left arm just below the shoulder. Rescuers wrapped a cord around the stump of her arm. She spent a week in the hospital. Three weeks after the shark encounter, Bethany returned to surfing.

Great white sharks can have as many as 3,000 teeth in their jaws at any given time.

Extra eyelids close when a shark bites down. They provide protection from thrashing prey.

The mako shark can swim 60 miles (96.6 km) per hour in short bursts.

Young sharks taste nearly everything to learn what is good to eat.

The 16-foot-long (4.9 m) big-eyed thresher shark has eyes the size of baseballs.

Some sharks can hear sounds more than half a mile (0.8 km) away.

Sharks are resistant to most diseases. They rarely get cancer.

Bull sharks are common in Florida's Everglades.

Tiger sharks can bite through the hard shells of sea turtles with ease

Sometimes strong pups eat weaker pups while still inside their mother's body.

A shark pup's greatest threat is a bigger shark.

Young hammerheads swim near the water's surface. This can cause sunburn.

Thresher sharks slap fish with their long tails. This knocks out the prey.

Great whites give birth

to as many as 12 pups every other year.

Xtreme Shark #1

Close Call In 2009, Paul de Gelder was swimming near Sydney Harbor. A bull shark grabbed Paul's leg and hand. It shook him like a dog shakes a toy. Then it let go and disappeared. Paul spent two months in the hospital. He lost his right forearm and leg. Today, Paul gives speeches and works with the Discovery Channel. He teaches people about the importance of sharks. He also dives with sharks and films them.

GLOSSARY

crustaceans – animals that have a hard shell and live in water

organs – parts of a living being that perform specific tasks in the body

parasites – animals or plants that live on or inside another living thing (called a host) while giving nothing back to the host; some parasites cause disease or even death

species – a group of living beings that are closely related

RESOURCES

Discovery Channel. *Sharkopedia: The Complete Guide to Everything Shark*. New York: Liberty Street, 2013.

"GPS for Sharks." University of Miami: R. J. Dunlap Marine Conservation Program. http://sharkresearch.rsmas.miami.edu/research/projects/gps-for-sharks.

Peschak, Thomas. P. *Sharks and People: Exploring Our Relationship with the Most Feared Fish in the Sea*. Chicago: University of Chicago, 2013.

"All About Sharks." Discovery Channel: Sharkopedia. http://sharkopedia.discovery.com/shark-topics/.

INDEX

The 18-foot (5.5 m) megamouth shark was discovered in 1976.